What is God's Purpose for Me?

A 4-week course to help **discover what God's** their lives.

By Steven B. Huddleston

Group®

Loveland, Colorado

Group

What Is God's Purpose for Me?

Copyright © 1992 Group Publishing, Inc.

Credits
Edited by Michael Warden
Cover designed by Jill Nordbye and DeWain Stoll
Interior designed by Judy Bienick and Jan Aufdemberge
Cover photo by Brenda Rundback
Illustrations by Raymond Medici

ISBN 1-55945-132-7

14 13 12 11 10 9 8 7 6   04 03 02 01 00 99 98 97 96
Printed in the United States of America.

CONTENTS

What Is God's Purpose for Me?

Who Am I?

Help junior highers recognize how their positive character traits can be used to serve God in their hobbies and future careers.

How Can I Make a Difference?

Help junior highers discover meaning for their lives by helping others.

Looking for God's Will

Help junior highers discover God's will for their lives.

Setting Priorities

Help junior highers set priorities and goals in their lives that will be pleasing to God and fulfilling to themselves.

WHAT IS GOD'S PURPOSE FOR ME?

"You've got to be kidding!" Allen's mother said in disbelief. The family doctor had just informed her that Allen's persistent stomach pains were the result of ulcers. "Ulcers?" she continued, "But he's only 12! How can a 12-year-old boy get ulcers?"

On the way home as she talked to her son, Allen's mom began to realize for the first time the tremendous pressures Allen had been under.

Allen had always dreamed of one day being a great singer. But when his voice began to change, Allen couldn't sing like he used to. He was even made fun of in music class at school. Meanwhile, his father had been pressuring him to join the football team so he would "carry on the family tradition." The only problem with that was Allen hated football.

Allen was also worried because his best friend's parents had just gotten a divorce. Allen's parents had been arguing a lot lately, and he was afraid his parents might split up too.

All of this led Allen to have serious questions about his identity and his purpose in life. He was feeling pressure to find a direction for his future, but everything he could see was a question mark. "Should I go ahead and play a game I hate, just so my dad won't be ashamed of me?... Is my family going to fall apart like so many others I see?... I can't sing anymore. What am I going to do with my life?"

While not every young person ends up with ulcers like Allen did, more and more young people feel pressured to make big decisions about life at an early age. Often, they make decisions based on peer pressure or parental expectations. And sometimes their sense of purpose is difficult to hang on to.

The church can help junior highers discover their identities and find a sense of purpose for their lives. By helping kids discover particular ways to contribute to their world and showing them how to determine God's will for their lives, you can challenge junior highers to re-think their priorities in light of their faith.

Then they can begin to recognize the possibilities for the future.

By the end of this course your students will:
- discover what makes them valuable and important;
- see what purpose there is with God in their future;
- recognize that serving others is one way to find purpose in their lives;
- learn how to set priorities in their lives; and
- develop mottos that will assist them in reaching their goals.

COURSE OBJECTIVES

HOW TO USE THIS COURSE

Think back on an important lesson you've learned in life. Did you learn it from reading about it? from hearing about it? from something you experienced? Chances are, the most important lessons you've learned came from something you've experienced. That's what active learning is—learning by doing. And active learning is a key element in Group's Active Bible Curriculum™.

Active learning leads students in doing things that help them understand important principles, messages and ideas. It's a discovery process that helps kids internalize what they learn.

Each lesson section in Group's Active Bible Curriculum™ plays an important part in active learning:

The **Opener** involves kids in the topic in fun and unusual ways.

The **Action and Reflection** includes an experience designed to evoke specific feelings in the students. This section also processes those feelings through "How did you feel?" questions and applies the message to situations kids face.

The **Bible Application** actively connects the topic with the Bible. It helps kids see how the Bible is relevant to the situations they face.

The **Commitment** helps students internalize the Bible's message and commit to making changes in their lives.

The **Closing** funnels the lesson's message into a time of creative reflection and prayer.

When you put all the sections together, you get a lesson that's fun to teach. And kids get messages they'll remember.

● Read the introduction, the Course Objectives and This Course at a Glance.

● Decide how you'll publicize the course using the clip art on the Publicity Page (p. 9). Prepare fliers, newsletter articles and posters as needed.

● Look at the Bonus Ideas (p. 39) and decide which ones you'll use.

• Read the opening statements, Objectives and Bible Basis for the lesson. The Bible Basis shows how specific passages relate to junior highers and middle schoolers today.

• Choose which Opener and Closing options to use. Each is appropriate for a different kind of group.

• Gather necessary supplies from This Lesson at a Glance.

• Read each section of the lesson. Adjust where necessary for your class size and meeting room.

• The approximate minutes listed give you an idea of how long each activity will take. Each lesson is designed to take 35 to 60 minutes. Shorten or lengthen activities as needed to fit your group.

• If you see you're going to have extra time, do an activity or two from the "If You Still Have Time . . . " box or from the Bonus Ideas (p. 39).

• Dive into the activities with the kids. Don't be a spectator. The lesson will be more successful and rewarding to both you and your students.

• Though some kids may at first think certain activities are "silly," they'll enjoy them and they'll remember the messages from these activities long after the lesson is over. As one Active Bible Curriculum™ user has said, "I can ask the kids questions about a lesson I did three weeks ago, and they actually remember what I taught!" And that's the whole idea of teaching . . . isn't it?

Have fun with the activities you lead. Remember, it is Jesus who encourages us to become "like little children." Besides, how often do your kids get *permission* to express their childlike qualities?

HELPFUL HINTS

• The answers given after discussion questions are responses your students *might* give. They aren't the only answers or the "right" answers. If needed, use them to spark discussion. Kids won't always say what you wish they'd say. That's why some of the responses given are negative or controversial. If someone responds negatively, don't be shocked. Accept the person and use the opportunity to explore other angles of the issue.

THIS COURSE AT A GLANCE

Before you dive into the lessons, familiarize yourself with each lesson aim. Then read the scripture passages.
- Study them as a background to the lessons.
- Use them as a basis for your personal devotions.
- Think about how they relate to kids' circumstances today.

LESSON 1: WHO AM I?

Lesson Aim: To help junior highers recognize how their positive character traits can be used to serve God in their hobbies and future careers.

Bible Basis: 1 Corinthians 12:12-20.

LESSON 2: HOW CAN I MAKE A DIFFERENCE?

Lesson Aim: To help junior highers discover meaning for their lives by helping others.

Bible Basis: Matthew 5:41—6:4 and James 1:26-27.

LESSON 3: LOOKING FOR GOD'S WILL

Lesson Aim: To help junior highers discover God's will for their lives.

Bible Basis: 2 Timothy 3:16-17 and James 1:5-6.

LESSON 4: SETTING PRIORITIES

Lesson Aim: To help junior highers set priorities and goals in their lives that will be pleasing to God and fulfilling to themselves.

Bible Basis: Matthew 22:35-40 and Philippians 3:10-14.

PUBLICITY PAGE

Grab your junior highers' attention! Photocopy this page, and then cut out and paste the clip art of your choice in your church bulletin or newsletter to advertise this course on finding God's purpose in life. Or photocopy and use the ready-made flier as a bulletin insert. Permission to photocopy clip art is granted for local church use.

Splash the clip art on posters, fliers or even postcards! Just add the vital details: the date and time the course begins and where you'll meet.

It's that simple.

What is *God's Purpose for Me?*

What is *God's Purpose for Me?*

What is *God's Purpose for Me?*

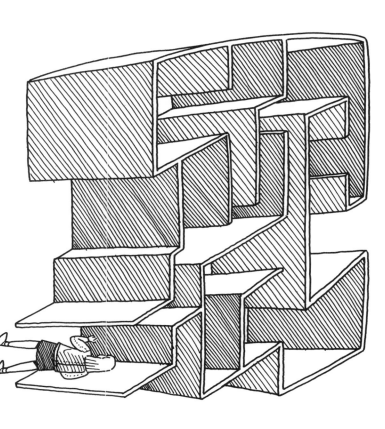

What is GOD'S PURPOSE FOR ME?

A 4-week junior high and middle school course on discovering God's purpose in life

Come to _____

On _____

At _____

Come explore together the things in life that really matter!

WHO AM I?

Junior highers sometimes feel like "ugly ducklings," unable to recognize their unique and special qualities. We can help them discover those God-given qualities that make them valuable and important to God and their world.

To help junior highers recognize how their positive character traits can be used to serve God in their hobbies and future careers.

Students will:
- **recognize their own character qualities and abilities that make them unique and special;**
- **identify possible careers and activities in which their qualities and abilities can be used to serve God;**
- **discover that their gifts and abilities are important to God's kingdom; and**
- **list hobbies and careers, and then develop a dream of how their abilities can be used for God in the future.**

Look up the following scriptures. Then read the background paragraphs to see how the passage relates to your junior highers and middle schoolers.

In **1 Corinthians 12:12-20**, Paul talks to the Corinthians about the body of Christ.

Paul saw how the misuse of spiritual gifts in Corinth had led to confusion. By describing the church as Christ's body—with every member playing its part—he hoped to help the Corinthians understand how it was wrong to exalt one part of Christ's body over another part. He wanted them to see how they could have unity in diversity.

Junior highers can learn from these verses that God gives each person gifts and abilities to use for God's purposes. Kids need to see that in Christ's body, there is no "pecking order," but each person has his or her place, according to the gifts and abilities God has given.

LESSON 1

LESSON AIM

OBJECTIVES

BIBLE BASIS
1 CORINTHIANS 12:12-20

Section	Minutes	What Students Will Do	Supplies
Opener (Option 1)	5 to 10	**Quality Inspection**—Begin to discover their talents.	"Quality Inspection" handouts (p. 18), pencils
(Option 2)		**Who Am I?**—Listen to clues to identify mystery characters.	Bibles, background information on one student
Action and Reflection	15 to 20	**Identity Crisis**—Discover their own "hidden identity" by asking classmates "yes" or "no" questions, then hear more about their positive character traits from others.	Nametags, pins or tape, pencils, 3×5 cards
Bible Application	10 to 15	**Body Parts**—Work with a group to create a "body," then perform a task.	Bible, blindfolds
Commitment	5 to 10	**Dream On**—Create a vision or dream of how they might use their abilities for God in the future.	Paper, pencils
Closing (Option 1)	up to 5	**For You, God**—Ask God to help them use their abilities to make a difference.	Posterboard or newsprint, cross, tape, markers
(Option 2)		**Nobody Without Him**—Listen to a song, and discuss how it applies to discovering who they are.	Taped song, tape deck

The Lesson

OPENER

(5 to 10 minutes)

☐ OPTION 1: QUALITY INSPECTION

Give a copy of the "Quality Inspection" handout (p. 18) to each student. Say: **There are several ways to determine what your gifts, talents and abilities are. Take a minute to complete the handout. It will help you get an idea of your areas of strength.**

After five minutes, have volunteers share parts of what they wrote on their handouts and explain why they responded as they did. Then say: **All of us have characteristics that make us unique and special. Today we're going to explore how valuable these abilities are and how important it is to put them to use for God.**

☐ OPTION 2: WHO AM I?

Form teams of four or five and give each team a Bible. Say: **Before we start today's lesson, I need you to help me figure out who I am. I'm going to read a list of qualities and facts and see which team can name the person I'm describing.**

Use the biographies that follow giving one clue at a time, or create your own.

Who am I? . . . I was born about 1120 B.C. . . . My father's name was Manoah . . . An angel told my mother before I was born that I was to be a Nazarite . . . I once baffled people with this riddle: "Out of the eater, something to eat; out of the strong, something sweet." . . . I once killed a thousand Philistines with a donkey's jawbone . . . I was in love with a woman named Delilah . . . When my hair was cut I lost my strength . . .

If students still do not know, let them use their Bibles to find the answer to the last clue: **My name can be found in Judges 15:16.** (Answer: Samson).

Who am I? . . . During a drought, God saw to it that I was fed by ravens . . . When God sent me to a widow to be fed, he multiplied her flour and oil so it would not be used up so there would be plenty for us to eat each day . . . When this widow's son fell sick and stopped breathing, God used me to bring the boy back to life . . . When I challenged the priests of Baal on Mt. Carmel, Jehovah brought fire upon my sacrifice, but the priests of Baal failed . . . I never died because I was miraculously taken by God in chariots of fire into heaven . . .

If students still do not know, let them use their Bibles to find the answer to the last clue: **My name can be found in 1 Kings 17:1.** (Answer: Elijah).

Before class gather information about one of the students in your group for the last "Who Am I?". Use this information to describe him or her. Use biographical information, but also include personality traits and talents. Be sure to use only information and descriptions that affirm the young person.

After all people are identified, congratulate the winning team or teams, then ask:

● **How did you feel as you heard the descriptions and tried to figure out the mystery people?** (Lost, I didn't know much about them; good, I knew them right away.)

● **Was it harder to guess the Bible characters or your classmate? Explain.** (The Bible characters, I don't know as much about them as I know about my classmate; my classmate, I didn't know those details of my classmate's life.)

● **How was determining the characters in this game like the struggle we sometimes have in determining our own abilities and talents?** (I sometimes feel lost because I don't know what makes me unique; good, I know myself well and figuring my abilities is easy.)

Say: **All of us like to feel comfortable in knowing who we are and how we're unique and special. Today we'll discover some things about ourselves that make us valuable and important to God.**

IDENTITY CRISIS

Pin or tape a nametag on each student's back with the name of a famous person or fictional character written on it. Don't let students see the nametag you're putting on them. Explain to the students that they're each to mingle around the room and ask questions to discover their own "hidden identity." Tell them they can't ask the same person two questions in a row, and all questions must be answered with a simple "yes" or "no."

After kids have each discovered the name on their nametag, call everyone together and ask:

● **How did you feel when you didn't know your "identity"?** (Curious; confused.)

● **Was it hard for you to discover the name on your back? Why or why not?** (Yes, I didn't know much about the person; no, the person had such a unique quality I got it right away.)

● **How is this activity like the struggle we sometimes face in trying to develop a sense of identity?** (I sometimes get confused or don't know how others see me; it's hard for me to see how I'm different from others.)

Say: **You each had to interact with others to discover your nametag identity. In the same way, we need others to help us discover who we are and to identify the things about us that make us special or unique.**

Form groups of four, and distribute pencils and 3×5 cards.

Say: **Have the person in your group whose birthday is coming next start as "It." I'll read a statement and give a choice of four answers. Choose and write on your card the answer you think best describes the person who's It. Your group will select a different person to be It for each statement I read.**

Here are the statements:

1. When this person becomes an adult he or she is more likely to be (a) a farmer; (b) a chemist; (c) a TV news anchorperson; or (d) a deep-sea diver.

2. This person would be best at helping a person who (a) needs help with his or her homework; (b) can't get his or her car started; (c) has just lost a close friend; or (d) needs someone to do his or her cooking.

3. If this person were an animal, he or she would be (a) an owl because of his or her wisdom; (b) a bunny because of his or her tenderness and warmth; (c) an ox because of his or her strength; or (d) a beaver because of his or her desire to work a lot.

4. If this person were a household appliance he or she would be (a) a radio because he or she can give lots of information; (b) a television because he or she is so entertaining; (c) a microwave because he or she knows how to save time and make everything easier; or (d) a toaster because he or she is so good at warming up to people.

After students each fill out their card, have group members compare their answers to see which person received the most matches. Then have group members explain why they answered as they did.

Ask:

● **What did you learn about yourself from the answers your group members gave?** (I learned that others think I'm easy to talk to; I found out that others think I'm a hard worker.)

● **How did you feel as others were describing you?** (Surprised, I didn't know others recognize that characteristic in me; challenged, to live up to the way others described me.)

Have group members each tell the person across from them one additional positive characteristic in that person that makes him or her special or unique.

BODY PARTS

Say: **By now you should be getting a pretty good idea of what some of your abilities and personality characteristics are and how you might be able to use them. God's Word tells us that all of us have gifts and abilities we can use in God's service, and all of these abilities are equally important in God's eyes. He needs and uses them all.**

Have a volunteer read 1 Corinthians 12:12-20. Have kids form groups of five. Tell them each group is to form one "body." Designate each of the following body parts to one person in each group: legs, eyes, right arm, left arm, and brain. Blindfold all group members except the "eyes." Explain to groups each that the eyes will read a task for the body to do, then communicate the task to the body by whispering it to the brain, who relays the message to the rest of the body parts. Each body part then does its role in completing the task. The legs must lead the way, and the arms must perform the task.

For example, the directions might be for the body to go down the hall to the closet, find the broom and sweep up a pile of trash you've placed there. Give each body a different task and see which one can complete its task first. When all groups are finished, ask:

● **How did you feel while carrying out your assignment?** (Frustrated, I could only do one thing to help; excited, we were able to work together.)

● **How does this experience relate to the abilities and character traits we each possess?** (Whatever our abilities are, they're important to the body of Christ; we can stifle the work God wants to do in us if we don't find ways to use our abilities.)

DREAM ON

Now that kids have had an opportunity to determine some of the abilities that make them important and valuable, ask them to think of possible careers or hobbies in which those abilities could be used for God. Hand out paper and pencils and have kids record their ideas. Then have them each use their list to create a word-picture "dream" or vision of how their abilities might be used for God in their future career.

After five minutes, form pairs and have kids each relate their dream to their partner. Have partners pray for each other, that they would never fall short of God's best dream for their lives.

After kids pray, say: **Take your dreams home with you as a reminder to keep your commitment to reach for God's dreams for your life.**

Table Talk

The Table Talk activity in this course helps junior highers and middle schoolers discuss with their parents how they can find purpose in life.

If you choose to use the Table Talk activity, this is a good time to show students the "Table Talk" handout (p. 19). Ask them to spend time with their parents completing it.

Before kids leave, give them each the "Table Talk" handout to take home, or tell them you'll be sending it to their parents. Tell kids to be prepared to report on their experience with the handout next week.

Or use the Table Talk idea found in the Bonus Ideas (p. 41) for a meeting based on the handout.

CLOSING
(up to 5 minutes)

☐ OPTION 1: FOR YOU, GOD

Before class, make a cross out of posterboard or newsprint and tape it to the wall. Have kids take turns writing on the cross one quality they possess that they'll use for God.

Take the cross off the wall and place it on the floor. Form a circle around the cross, and close in prayer, asking God to help students use the abilities they listed to make a difference in their world.

☐ OPTION 2: NOBODY WITHOUT HIM

Form a circle and turn off the lights. Play the song "Who Am I?" by Margaret Becker from her album *The Reckoning* (Sparrow Records).

After the song, leave the lights off, and ask:
● **How does the message of this song relate to what we've talked about today?** (Without God we are nothing; we're special because of Christ's spirit living in us.)
● **How can the message of this song help us in discovering who we are and how we can live for God?** (We need to go to God to understand why we're so special; even though we're special, we need to stay humble.)

Close with prayer, thanking God for the life of his son that makes each of us special in a unique way.

If You Still Have Time . . .

Buried Talents—Have students read Matthew 25:14-30 silently. Then choose one volunteer to narrate, one to read the words of the master and three volunteers to read the words of the three servants. Point out how our talents are also gifts from God, and discuss the importance of using the talents our heavenly master has entrusted to us.

Talent Tower—Form teams of five and give each team markers, a stack of 3×5 cards and masking tape. On "go," have teams compete to see which one can build the tallest "talent tower." On each card, write an ability or positive character trait of a member of the team. Then tape the card to the wall. The first card must be touching the ground. Each succeeding card must touch the previous card, thus constructing a "tower."

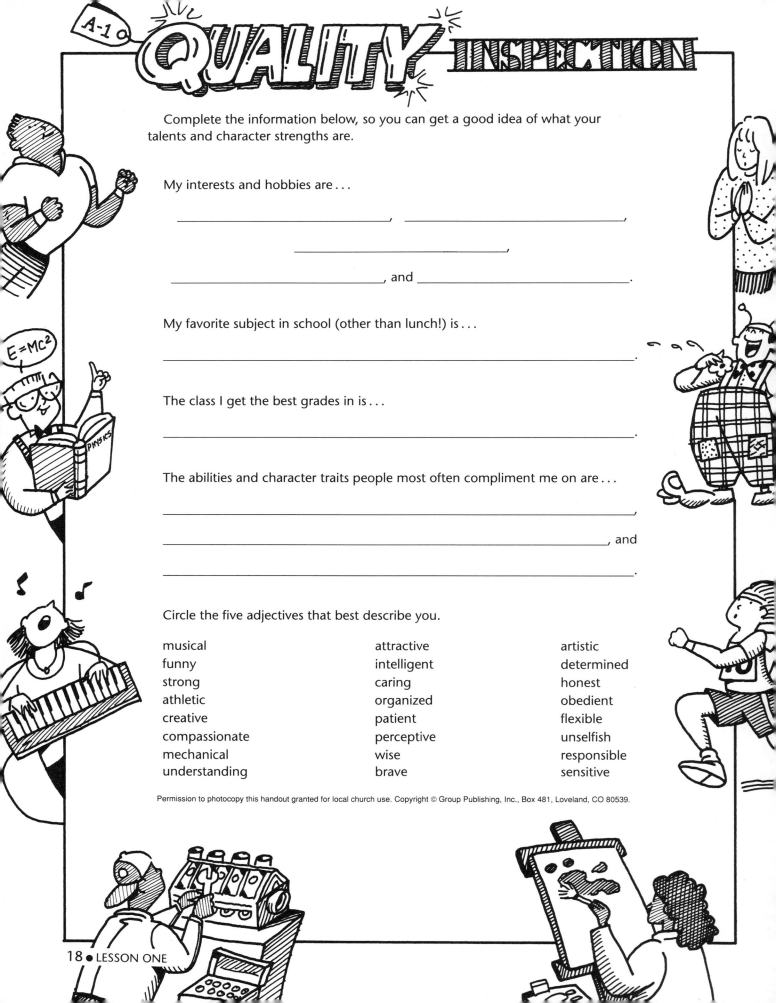

QUALITY INSPECTION

A-1

Complete the information below, so you can get a good idea of what your talents and character strengths are.

My interests and hobbies are . . .

_____, _____,

_____,

_____, and _____.

My favorite subject in school (other than lunch!) is . . .

_____.

The class I get the best grades in is . . .

_____.

The abilities and character traits people most often compliment me on are . . .

_____

_____, and

_____.

Circle the five adjectives that best describe you.

musical	attractive	artistic
funny	intelligent	determined
strong	caring	honest
athletic	organized	obedient
creative	patient	flexible
compassionate	perceptive	unselfish
mechanical	wise	responsible
understanding	brave	sensitive

Table Talk

To the Parent: We're involved in a junior high course at church called *What Is God's Purpose for Me?* Students are exploring what makes them valuable and important and how they can contribute to their world. We'd like you and your junior higher to spend some time discussing this important topic. Use this "Table Talk" page to help you do that.

Parents

Respond to each of the following statements or questions:
- When you were in junior high school, what did you imagine your life would be like?
- What goals did you set for yourself when you graduated from high school?
- Did you reach these goals? Why or why not?
- How has your relationship with God played a role in the setting and reaching of your goals?
- Describe what your dreams and goals are for the future.

Junior higher

Respond to each of the following statements or questions:
- Describe your future life and the talents and characteristics you hope to develop.
- What goals do you have right now for school, extra-curricular activities and a career?
- Describe steps you plan to take to help you reach those goals.
- What role does God play in the goals you have set and in how you plan to achieve them?

Parent and junior higher

Follow these instructions together:
- Tell one talent or characteristic that you admire in each other.
- Set a goal together for serving God. List objectives toward achieving this goal. Set priorities that'll help you succeed.
- Pray together that God will help you with your joint goal as well as with your individual goals and dreams.

HOW CAN I MAKE A DIFFERENCE?

Today's teenagers are tomorrow's world leaders. Yet many young people don't recognize they can make a significant contribution to society. We can help kids envision ways they can serve others and make a difference in their world.

LESSON AIM

To help junior highers discover meaning for their lives by helping others.

OBJECTIVES

Students will:
- **discover ways to use their talents to help others;**
- **see that serving others is one way to find purpose in life; and**
- **explore biblical examples of people who used their talents to help others.**

BIBLE BASIS

MATTHEW 5:41—6:4
JAMES 1:26-27

Look up the following scriptures. Then read the background paragraphs to see how the passages relate to your junior highers and middle schoolers.

In **Matthew 5:41—6:4**, Jesus gives instructions about helping others.

In this passage, Jesus confronts the pride and hypocrisy in people that keeps them from helping those around them in a way that's pleasing to God. He challenges his listeners to love their enemies, do good to those who hate them and to be sure their aid to the poor is done in secret.

Jesus' words may seem radical to junior highers—because they are! But kids need to understand how committed Jesus is to loving people and serving them, so that they too can follow in his footsteps.

In **James 1:26-27**, James defines the kind of "religion" that God accepts.

In these verses, James summarizes the few, simple things that God requires of all those who would worship in an acceptable way. The writer strips away all of the "baggage" that modern religions can carry and exposes the heart of what it means to love God.

In our culture, kids may not always be conscious of people in need. Nevertheless, people with needs are all around us. Junior highers can learn to "see" the widows and orphans in their own communities and reach out to them.

THIS LESSON AT A GLANCE

Section	Minutes	What Students Will Do	Supplies
Opener (Option 1) (Option 2)	5 to 10	**Recipe for Success**—List what they think are the needed ingredients for success. **Quick Change Artist**—Identify subtle changes in their partner's appearance.	Newsprint, markers
Action and Reflection	15 to 20	**Quality Auction**—"Purchase" talents, then think of ways to use those talents to help a young girl in need.	Paper, marker
Bible Application	10 to 15	**A Handful of Helpers**—Look up scriptures to discover how some people in the Bible used their abilities to help others.	"A Handful of Helpers" handouts (p. 25), pencils, Bibles
Commitment	5 to 10	**Ability Ads**—Create a poster advertisement of one of their talents or character traits.	Posterboard, old magazines, glue, markers
Closing (Option 1) (Option 2)	up to 5	**Opportunity Knocks**—Identify a specific individual's need they can help meet in the coming week. **Poster Mural**—Create a mural of the whole youth group's talents and abilities.	3×5 cards, pencils Ads, newsprint, markers, tape

The Lesson

☐ OPTION 1: RECIPE FOR SUCCESS

Before class, mount a sheet of newsprint on the wall with the following words at the top: "To be a real success in the world, you need . . . " As students enter the room, have them use markers to write on the newsprint as many answers as they can think of.

Move into the lesson by looking at the list and pointing out that throughout history, people with vastly different backgrounds and qualities have been "successful."

Say: **Today, we'll look at ways God can use each of us with our varying abilities to make a difference in the lives of other people.**

☐ OPTION 2: QUICK CHANGE ARTIST

Have students find a partner and face each other. Then tell partners to turn and stand back-to-back. On your signal, have kids each change something about their appearance, then turn around and try to guess what their partner changed. Have kids exchange partners and try it a few more times.

Say: **Sometimes the little things we do go unnoticed and seem unimportant. But today we're going to look at ways God can use us to make a difference that will matter in the lives of others.**

Table Talk Follow-Up

If you sent the "Table Talk" handout (p. 19) to parents last week, discuss students' reactions to the activity. Ask volunteers to share what they learned from the discussion with their parents.

QUALITY AUCTION

Before class, take several sheets of paper and list one talent or character trait in large letters on each sheet; for example, a great singing voice, an athletic body, a pretty face, a quick mind, honesty, loyalty or sincerity. List some traits that are valuable from a worldly perspective as well as some that are valuable from a Christian perspective.

Explain that there will be an auction, and kids will each be allotted $1,000 to spend on the various traits and talents to be auctioned off. Hold up the first sheet of paper, and begin the bidding for that particular trait or talent. Give the sheet of paper to the highest bidder who will then subtract the purchase price from his or her $1,000 total.

Continue until all the traits and talents are auctioned off or until all the money is gone.

After the auction, form groups of four or five and have kids hang on to their purchases while you say: **Let me tell you about a girl named Lisa. Lisa is an eighth-grader at Oak Junior High.**

Last night Lisa's house burned down. She lost all her possessions. She's the only member of her family to survive the blaze. Right now, Lisa is in the hospital with painful burns that will scar her for life.

Have group members share with one another ways the traits or talents they purchased could be used to help Lisa.

After they've shared with their groups, ask:

● **How did you feel as you looked for ways to use your character qualities to help Lisa?** (Bad, the traits I bought wouldn't be much help to her; glad, I bought a trait that could really help Lisa.)

● **How was this exercise like the traits or talents we seek and obtain in real life?** (Sometimes the traits we long for in life aren't as valuable as we think they are; different traits are needed in different situations.)

● **How does this experience apply to you today?** (Instead of wishing for other traits, I should be finding ways to use the traits I do have; I need to stop wishing for qualities that really don't matter.)

Say: **From this experience, we can see that there are lots of character traits that people find valuable. But God wants us to develop those traits that can be used to help others.**

A HANDFUL OF HELPERS

Distribute one "A Handful of Helpers" handout (p. 25) to each group, along with a pencil and a Bible. Have students work in their groups from the last activity to complete the handout. After about ten minutes, have two volunteers read aloud Matthew 5:41—6:4 and James 1:26-27.

Ask:

● **What do the biblical examples in all of these passages say about the way we're supposed to live?** (They tell us to take advantage of the opportunities we have to help others; they help us remember to use our abilities to help all people, not just a select few.)

● **If you did what these verses command 100 percent of the time, how would your life be different?** (I wouldn't spend so much time doing things just for myself; I would be a lot more loving toward others.)

Say: **Serving others is a key part of Christ's message for life. As we learn to give to others the way Jesus does, we'll discover the joy of living unselfishly, and we'll become more like Jesus.**

BIBLE APPLICATION
(10 to 15 minutes)

COMMITMENT
(5 to 10 minutes)

CLOSING
(up to 5 minutes)

ABILITY ADS

Say: **Let's take some positive steps toward helping others more.**

Have students use posterboard, old magazines, glue and markers to create "advertisements" of one or more of their talents and positive character traits. Have kids each draw two circles in the middle of their ad and leave them blank.

After several minutes, have volunteers explain their ads.

Say: **In one of the blank circles on your ad, write one "guarantee" of how you'll use this talent or ability to help others this week.**

Form pairs, and have kids explain their guarantees to their partners.

Then say: **Take your partner's ad and in the remaining blank circle, write an additional talent or character trait *you* see in that person that makes him or her valuable to others.**

When pairs have finished, have kids write their names on their ads, then collect them to hang on the walls at a later time.

Encourage kids each to check during the week to see if their partner is following through on their guarantee.

☐ OPTION 1: OPPORTUNITY KNOCKS

Hand out 3×5 cards and pencils. Have kids each write the name of a person they know who has a need that he or she can meet.

Form a circle, and have kids hold their cards out in front of them. Close with prayer, asking God to help kids start fulfilling their "guarantees" with the people on the cards this week.

☐ OPTION 2: POSTER MURAL

Clear a large space on the wall. Redistribute kids' poster ads (from the commitment activity), along with newsprint, markers and tape. Have kids work together to create a mural that represents all the good things the youth group has to offer the people in the community. Have kids think of an appropriate title that deals with serving others.

Close with prayer, thanking God for giving kids the talents and abilities they need to help others.

If You Still Have Time . . .

Together We Serve—Have group members brainstorm ways they can work together to make a difference at their schools or in their communities. Write kids' ideas on newsprint, and choose one to do as a group within the next two months.

Someone Special—Ask students to each tell the group about a person who has been especially helpful in their life. Have them discuss why these people have been so helpful and what they can learn from these individuals about using our abilities to help others.

A HANDFUL OF HELPERS

Look up the scriptures to complete the chart below:

Scripture	Who helped	Talent or character trait used	How it was used to help others
1 Samuel 16:23			
Luke 10:30-35			
Acts 4:32-37			
Philemon 4-7			

LESSON 3

LOOKING FOR GOD'S WILL

Perhaps more than ever before, young people are being pushed to make many tough decisions in life at a young age. The struggles to make the right choices can be difficult and stressful. Fortunately, we can offer junior highers help by showing them ways to find guidance from God in the decisions they make.

LESSON AIM

To help junior highers discover God's will for their lives.

OBJECTIVES

Students will:
- discover the value in following God's will;
- explore ways to seek God's will through prayer, scripture and counsel from other Christians;
- recognize that God's will never involves disobeying instructions in the Bible; and
- seek to follow God's will more closely.

BIBLE BASIS

2 TIMOTHY 3:16-17
JAMES 1:5-6

Look up the following scriptures. Then read the background paragraphs to see how the passages relate to your junior highers and middle schoolers.

In **2 Timothy 3:16-17**, Paul tells Timothy that scripture is inspired by God.

Timothy was a young man who was sometimes in stressful situations. Even though God's blessing was upon him, he needed guidance to know what to do. Paul told him he needed to look no further than the Bible, which contains the living, inspired counsel of God.

Junior highers want to find answers to the problems they face, but they often don't go to the right places to find those answers. The Bible can provide them with the direction they need to make choices that are pleasing to God.

In **James 1:5-6**, James reminds his fellow Christians that God freely gives wisdom to those who ask.

James understood that God allows hard times in our lives so that we might gain wisdom. He knew that it is God's desire that we become wise, so we can live in a way that's pleasing to God and fulfilling for us.

Like the rest of us, kids need to understand that God does not want them to have to guess what's right and wrong or which direction they should go in life. They need to see that wisdom is available to all who ask for it with a teachable heart.

THIS LESSON AT A GLANCE

Section	Minutes	What Students Will Do	Supplies
Opener (Option 1)	5 to 10	**Finish the Story**—Finish an open-ended story about two boys and a cave.	
(Option 2)		**Father, May I?**—Respond to a list of statements by indicating how strongly they agree or disagree that the action is God's will.	"Strongly Agree" sign, "Strongly Disagree" sign
Action and Reflection	15 to 20	**Guidance Hide-ance**—Experience how it feels to be assigned a task and not know how to accomplish it.	"Guidance Hide-ance" handout (p. 32), scissors
Bible Application	10 to 15	**How God Guides**—Identify ways to determine God's will.	Bibles, paper, pencils, newsprint, markers
Commitment	5 to 10	**Piece-ful Prayer**—Devise a reminder to pray frequently for God's guidance in specific areas of their lives.	Puzzle pieces from the Action and Reflection activity, pencils
Closing (Option 1)	up to 5	**Stray Sheep**—Recognize areas of sin in their lives, and ask for forgiveness.	Bible, paper, pencils
(Option 2)		**Protection and Provision**—Reflect on God's protection and provision in their lives.	

The Lesson

☐ OPTION 1: FINISH THE STORY

Read the following story to the class: **Kirk and Todd were in the mood for adventure. They were familiar with the old town legend that a treasure was hidden deep inside the old Hollow Fork Cave. Today, they decided, would be the day they found that old treasure. If they had bothered**

OPENER
(5 to 10 minutes)

to ask their parents, they would have been warned not to go near the dangerous cave—but they didn't ask. On the way to Hollow Fork, they met Mr. Reeves, an old man and family friend. When he asked the boys where they were off to, they just said they were going exploring. Had they mentioned to Mr. Reeves their intentions to go in the old cave, he could have explained to them how the myth of the treasure was started years ago. He could even have told them how his own brother was killed in that very cave when they were boys. But they never gave him a chance to warn them. As Kirk and Todd entered the mouth of the cave, they walked right past a big sign. If they had taken the time to read it, they would have learned that the cave was prone to rapid and dangerous flooding. But they didn't bother to read the sign. Kirk and Todd went into the cave armed only with their flashlights.

After climbing and crawling between rocks for about an hour, they suddenly heard a strange noise . . .

Stop reading, form pairs and give pairs three to five minutes to decide the story ending and its consequences with their partners.

When time is up, have pairs each share their story ending and its consequences. Discuss the motives for the warnings and the various ways the two boys could have avoided the consequences.

Say: **When we neglect to follow God's instructions and warnings for our lives, we are apt to suffer consequences also. Today, we're going to look at ways to seek and follow God's will for our lives.**

☐ OPTION 2: FATHER, MAY I?

Have students stand in a single file line with a "Strongly Agree" sign posted on the wall at one end of the room and a "Strongly Disagree" sign posted at the other end.

Read the following list of statements (or create your own list). After reading a statement, have students each move to the spot in the line which best reflects their opinion of that statement.

Say: **It is God's will for you to . . .**
- **go to church even if you don't get anything out of it.**
- **have sex before marriage if you really love each other.**
- **avoid anyone at school who isn't a Christian.**
- **go to youth meetings even if it means getting a zero on your homework the next day.**
- **listen to rock music.**
- **tell a "white lie" if you're trying to avoid hurting someone else's feelings.**

As you read the statements, occasionally ask kids to explain why they believe the way they do.

Say: **Sometimes determining God's will is difficult to**

do. Today, we're going to explore different ways to know and follow God's plan for our lives.

GUIDANCE HIDE-ANCE

Before class, make four copies of the "Guidance Hide-ance" puzzle handout (p. 32) and cut out the puzzle pieces from three of the handouts.

Form at least three teams with each team getting a stack of puzzle pieces from one handout. Say: **When the pieces are arranged properly, they'll reveal something God gives to every believer. Let's see which team can put the puzzle together first.**

Students will almost certainly not be able to solve the puzzle. After a few moments of frustration, give a copy of the handout with the directions to one of the teams. Whisper to the team members that when they have solved the puzzle, they may verbally tell *one* other team the secret, *if* another team asks them.

After several minutes, ask:

● **How did you feel during this exercise? Explain.** (Frustrated, I couldn't figure out how to put the puzzle together; excited, it was a fun challenge.)

● **How did you feel when I gave your team the directions?** (Relieved; sorry for the other teams that didn't have them.)

● **How did it feel to be told the answer by another team? Explain.** (Grateful, they helped us; disappointed, we couldn't do it on our own.)

● **How did it feel to be left in the dark while other groups knew the key? Explain.** (Angry, they had help and we didn't; left out, we weren't told anything.)

● **How is this activity like trying to figure out God's will?** (It's hard to figure it out on your own; it's easier to figure out God's will when you have the Bible or help from someone else to guide you.)

● **How can you apply this to your life today?** (I can read the Bible more to help me determine God's will; I can listen to other Christians who have been in a similar situation before.)

Say: **Life can be a lot like this puzzle. But God has given us instructions through the Bible and the Holy Spirit so that we can better understand the "big picture."**

HOW GOD GUIDES

Form groups of four, and assign each group one of these two passages: 2 Timothy 3:16-17 or James 1:5-6. Give each group a Bible, a sheet of paper and a pencil. Tell groups each to discover and write what their passage says about finding God's will.

When groups are finished, ask them to share their answers with the rest of the class. Write groups' responses on newsprint.

ACTION AND REFLECTION
(15 to 20 minutes)

BIBLE APPLICATION
(10 to 15 minutes)

Ask:

- **How do these methods relate to the puzzle activity we did earlier?** (Reading the Bible is like looking at the directions; listening to the counsel of others is like being told by the other group how to make it work.)
- **How does the Holy Spirit help us understand God's will?** (The Spirit speaks to us through the Bible or through people; the Spirit speaks to us in our hearts to tell us which way is right.)
- **What should you do when the Bible, people and what you feel in your heart don't agree?** (Look to the Bible first, it's never wrong; follow where you think God is leading you even if someone disagrees.)

Say: **Several ways are provided for us to find God's will for our lives. Working together as a whole, these ways almost always make a clear path for us to follow and help us know we are in God's will.**

PIECE-FUL PRAYER

Have someone read aloud Philippians 4:13 as a reminder that God doesn't tell us to do something without providing a way for us to do it. Have each student take a puzzle piece from the "Guidance Hide-ance" activity above. Have kids each write on their puzzle piece one area of their life that they need God's guidance. Tell students each to keep the puzzle piece in their pocket or place it where it can be seen often to serve as a frequent reminder to pray for guidance in that area of their life.

Say: **Let's pray silently now. As you pray, agree to follow God's will in this area of your life, whatever it is.**

☐ OPTION 1: STRAY SHEEP

Have a volunteer read aloud Isaiah 53:6. Give kids slips of paper and pencils. Have them each write one area in their life that's "gone their own way" and hasn't been completely God's will.

Form groups of three, and read aloud Isaiah 53:6 to the groups again. One at a time, have group members each throw their paper on the floor to represent their desire for the forgiveness that God offers through Christ.

As a closing, have kids tell one another one way they see that person following God's will. Then have groups close in prayer, giving thanks for wisdom to understand God's will for their lives.

☐ OPTION 2: PROTECTION AND PROVISION

Form pairs. Have partners share with each other one time they were protected from harm because they followed God's will. Then have them share one time they received a blessing

---

COMMITMENT
(5 to 10 minutes)

CLOSING
(up to 5 minutes)

they would've missed had they not followed God's will.

Close by having kids each tell their partner one way they see God's blessing on their life. Finish off with a prayer of thanks for God's protection and provision.

If You Still Have Time . . .

Command Performance—Tape a sheet of newsprint to the wall. Ask kids to "brainstorm" for one minute to see how many "dos" and "don'ts" from the Bible they can list. Then have students determine how each command can either protect us or provide for us. Write their answers on the newsprint next to the command.

Weave Through Chaos—Select a volunteer to blindfold and send through a maze of chairs. Divide the rest of the class evenly between those who give helpful instructions, and those who will try to lead the volunteer off the path. Discuss the many "voices" kids hear when they are searching for God's will, and determine how kids can sift through the voices to find God's guidance.

Emily ▶ Relationship with Luke.
Stephanie ▶ Use good judgement - not be grounded.
Melissa ▶ relationship with Sarah
Annie ▶ friend
▶

GUIDANCE HIDE-ANCE

Make one copy of this page for each team you have. Cut out the black shapes and give them to the teams as puzzle pieces. Make an extra copy of this page to give to one team for the directions.

SETTING PRIORITIES

I n a society that no longer emphasizes morals and values, junior highers can have a hard time determining what their priorities in life should be. We can make this task easier for young people as we help them develop a value system based on God's Word.

To help junior highers set priorities and goals in their lives that will be pleasing to God and fulfilling to themselves.

Students will:
- **understand the cost involved in going for a prize;**
- **recognize that all goals and priorities for their lives must be God-centered;**
- **determine God's most important priority for their lives; and**
- **commit to live according to God's priorities.**

Look up the following scriptures. Then read the background paragraphs to see how the passages relate to your junior highers and middle schoolers.

In **Matthew 22:35-40**, Jesus identifies the most important commandment.

The religious leaders of the Jews almost seemed to revel in the abundance of laws they followed in order to be "righteous." From all these, Jesus singles out loving God as the first and greatest commandment.

Junior highers are just beginning to wonder what's really important in life. As they learn to set priorities, they can benefit greatly by learning about the one thing that Jesus thought was the most important priority in life—loving God.

In **Philippians 3:10-14**, Paul explains the motivation

LESSON AIM

OBJECTIVES

BIBLE BASIS
MATTHEW 22:35-40
PHILIPPIANS 3:10-14

behind his ministry.

Paul knew exactly why he followed Christ. He knew the costs, and he understood the rewards. He had forsaken everything that made him who he was to become the person Christ had created him to be. And he did it all so he could know God and one day receive the "prize" that waited for him in heaven.

Just as Paul had a firm grasp on his purpose in life, junior highers also can find that sense of purpose for their lives in God. By looking at Paul's example, they too can discover the joy of living for Christ and look forward to the prize God has prepared for them in his presence.

THIS LESSON AT A GLANCE

Section	Minutes	What Students Will Do	Supplies
Opener (Option 1)	5 to 10	**Choose Your Prize**—Decide which activity to do, knowing the prizes are different for each one.	Gum
(Option 2)		**Quarantined**—Decide what one material object is most important to them.	
Action and Reflection	15 to 20	**Cookie Chaos**—Decide whether to go through several stations to gain a prize.	Bag of cookies, squirt guns, Life Savers candies, flour, small bowls, bucket, ice water, chalkboard, towels
Bible Application	10 to 15	**Top Priority**—Determine what the Christian's number one priority should be.	Tape, newsprint, markers, Bibles
Commitment	5 to 10	**First Things First**—Determine their five top priorities.	Paper, pencils
Closing (Option 1)	up to 5	**A Verse to Live By**—Choose a passage of scripture to help them remember their priorities.	Bibles, 3×5 cards, pencils
(Option 2)		**My Motto**—Decide on a personal motto to help them keep their priorities in order.	Chalkboard, chalk

The Lesson

OPENER
(5 to 10 minutes)

☐ OPTION 1: CHOOSE YOUR PRIZE

As kids enter, tell them each they must choose to do one of three things:

1. stand perfectly still for one minute;
2. make goofy faces for one minute; or
3. jump around like a wild monkey for one minute.

Explain that the more extreme the behavior, the greater the prize will be. Have kids make their choices and do their actions for one minute. Award those who stood still each with one piece of gum, those who made goofy faces each with two pieces of gum and those who jumped around each with three pieces of gum.

Ask:

● **Why did you choose the action you did?** (I wanted the prize; it sounded like fun.)

● **Were you pleased with what you got? Why or why not?** (No, I thought we should have gotten something more special; yes, I like this flavor of gum.)

● **How did your personal priorities play into your decision about which action to choose?** (I wanted the biggest prize, so I did the weirdest thing; I was embarrassed, so I just stood still.)

Say: **Our priorities affect almost everything we do each day, from what time we get up in the morning to what we watch on television. Today we're going to talk about how we can set priorities that are pleasing to God.**

☐ OPTION 2: QUARANTINED

Form groups of five or fewer. Ask students to imagine they've contracted a rare and deadly disease. They have only a few weeks to live, and they're so contagious that the doctors insist they stay in a sealed room until they die.

Ask:

● **If you could only take one material possession into that room with you, what would you choose, and why?**

Have students share their answers with their group members.

Say: **Sometimes our circumstances have a way of clarifying what's really important to us in life. Today, we're going to explore the priorities in our lives to make sure we're putting first things first.**

COOKIE CHAOS

Place a bag full of cookies at one end of the room and have students line up in a straight line at the other end of the room. Explain that anyone who makes it all the way across the room during the activity will get an even share of the cookies. But to cross the room, kids must agree to pass through a series of five stations.

One at a time, have kids proceed forward to station 1 and say, "(Leader's name) is awesome!" in order to go on. If a student won't say this, he or she is eliminated and forfeits his or her share of the cookies.

Here's what kids must do at the rest of the stations in order to go on:

● station 2—kids allow you to squirt water in their faces;

ACTION AND REFLECTION
(15 to 20 minutes)

● station 3—kids fish a Life Savers candy out of a bowl of flour using only their teeth;

● station 4—kids remove shoes and socks and place both feet in a bucket of ice water for 15 seconds; and

● station 5—kids scrape their fingernails across a chalkboard—twice.

Divide the cookies among those who went through all the stations. Ask:

● **Was it worth it? Why or why not?** (No, the cookies aren't even that great; yes, it was fun.)

● **Why did you keep going even when the requirements got more severe?** (I wanted the cookies; I was already committed.)

● **What were your priorities in this exercise?** (To get the cookies; to have fun.)

● **How did your priorities affect the way you approached this exercise?** (I didn't really care about the cookies, so I didn't go through all the stations; I really wanted the cookies, so I went through every station to get the prize.)

● **How might this experience apply to our faith?** (When living for Jesus is our priority, we're willing to go through a lot; as Christians, we should be willing to pay the price to know God.)

Say: **If something's important to us, we're willing to go through a lot to get it. So, as we set our faith in Christ and our Christian service high on our priority list, our lives will begin to reflect our devotion through the way we live.**

BIBLE APPLICATION
(10 to 15 minutes)

TOP PRIORITY

Tape a sheet of newsprint to the wall and title it "The Top Priority." Form pairs, and assign each pair one of these two passages: Matthew 22:35-40 or Philippians 3:10-14. Have pairs each race to look up and determine the "top priority" Christians should have based on their passage. As soon as pairs have an answer, have them race up to the newsprint, one pair at a time, and write it.

When all the pairs are finished, have the whole group work together to combine all their answers into one, unified top priority all Christians should have. Write that priority at the top of the newsprint.

Say: **Just as you each raced to discover God's top priority, so we each need to "race" to see how we can apply that priority to our lives from now on. Let's take time to do that now.**

COMMITMENT
(5 to 10 minutes)

FIRST THINGS FIRST

Distribute paper and pencils, and have students each list their top five priorities for this year. Then ask them to look at the top priority written on the newsprint, and alter, replace or eliminate those priorities that conflict with the top priority.

Ask:

● **How will including the top priority we wrote change the way you'll live this year?** (I'll spend more time at church; I won't hang around with the same friends anymore.)

● **Why will living this top priority be worth it?** (I want to follow God more than anything; I know God knows what's best for me.)

● **What's one thing you'll do this week to put your new priority into practice?** (I'll start doing my homework regularly; I'll read the Bible more often.)

Say: **By placing God as our number one priority, we'll not only start to bless others more, but we'll put ourselves in a place where we can receive God's best for us.**

☐ OPTION 1: A VERSE TO LIVE BY

Set out five Bibles around the room, with each Bible marked at one of the following verses: Philippians 3:14; Philippians 4:13; Colossians 2:6; Colossians 3:17; and 1 Peter 3:15-16. Choose five volunteers to go to the Bibles and take turns reading the marked verses to the class. After all the verses have been read, have students each decide which verse to use as a verse to live by. Have kids each go to the Bible verse of their choice and copy it onto a 3×5 card. Encourage them to memorize this verse during the week so it can be a constant help to them as they learn to live out their top priority.

Close with prayer, asking God to help kids live their lives fully for God.

☐ OPTION 2: MY MOTTO

Form groups of four and have group members work together to create a "motto" to help them with their priorities; for example, "Go for the prize; don't compromise." Write group mottos on the board as they share them with the class. Challenge kids each to pick one motto (or another if he or she has one in mind) and commit it to memory to use daily to help keep their priorities in order.

Close with prayer, thanking God for giving kids the courage to live their priorities. As an "amen," have kids all yell out their mottos at the same time!

CLOSING
(up to 5 minutes)

If You Still Have Time . . .

Just Like Jesus—Ask kids each to tell the group the name of their friend or relative who is most like Jesus and why.

Course Reflection—Form a circle. Ask students to reflect on the past four lessons. Have them take turns completing the following sentences:

● Something I learned in this course was . . .

● If I could tell my friends about this course, I'd say . . .

● Something I'll do differently because of this course is . . .

BONUS IDEAS

Bonus Scriptures—The lessons focus on a select few scripture passages, but if you'd like to incorporate more Bible readings into the lessons, here are our suggestions:
- **Psalm 119:1-40** (The author praises the wisdom of living according to God's Word.)
- **Isaiah 30:20-21** (Isaiah explains how God will direct the steps of his people.)
- **Jeremiah 29:11-13** (Jeremiah encourages God's people to realize God's plans for them are good.)
- **Romans 12:1-2** (Paul admonishes Christians to walk in God's will for their lives.)
- **1 Corinthians 13:1-7** (Paul explains that all things are meaningless without love.)
- **Ephesians 2:5-10** (Paul explains that God has prepared good things for his people to do.)

Ability in Action—Prepare a simple service project kids can do in the church building, such as cleaning nursery toys or washing the kitchen cupboards. Have students complete this project as a way to begin "making a difference."

Solve the Dilemma—Form groups of four and give each group a sheet of paper with a different "dilemma" described on it, each focusing on a young person struggling with his or her priorities. For example: "Chrystal really would like to grow in Christ, but she never seems to have time for devotions. She comes to you and says, 'Isn't it enough that I come to church every Sunday . . . well, almost every Sunday?' What would you tell Chrystal?" Have groups each decide what advice they would give to help solve their person's dilemma. Then have groups share their ideas with the rest of the class.

Three-Legged Wheelbarrow Race—Form teams of three for a relay race. Have two team members tie their legs together and hold up the legs of the third team member, who'll act as the "wheelbarrow." Place a chair about 20 feet away from each line. Have contestants race around the chairs and back to their team's line, so the next team can go. Time each team. The team with the best time wins.

When the race is over, discuss what the team's goals were in the race, and what objectives they had that helped them reach their goals. Discuss how this race applies to their goals in life and how they set priorities to reach those goals.

Mail Minder—Ask students each to fill out a commitment

MEETINGS AND MORE

card. Have them each write their choice of a helpful quality to develop in their life and their plan to develop that quality in the coming week. Have kids seal their completed cards in self-addressed envelopes, and collect them from the students. Four weeks later, mail the cards to students each as a reminder of their commitment.

In the Bubble—Create large air bubbles using window fans, plastic drop-cloths and duct tape. To make each bubble, tape two edges of the dropcloth to the floor, about three feet apart. Pleat and tape one end of the plastic to the window fan. Pleat and tape the other end to create an opening large enough for kids to crawl through. When the fan is turned on, the bubble will inflate. You'll need one bubble for every eight kids.

Have students form groups of eight and assign each group member one of these character roles: a 24-year-old pregnant woman; a 28-year-old male police officer who is a munitions expert; a 35-year-old male minister; a 36-year-old female doctor; a 46-year-old male farmer; a 74-year-old retired chemist with a bad heart; a 14-year-old female honor student; a 25-year-old male engineer.

Before groups enter their bubbles, explain the following scenario: The world has just experienced a freak collision with a huge meteor. The resulting radioactive dust cloud will span the globe. You and your companions are safe in the only known radiation proof fallout shelter. It is likely that you are the only survivors on Earth. Your biggest problem is that there is only enough oxygen for four people to survive in the bubble until the radiation outside has dissipated enough to make it safe to exit. In order to have survivors, four people must be cast out of the bubble. Your job is to decide in the next few minutes which of you will survive and which of you will be cast out.

Have groups decide among themselves who stays and who goes. Once a person is voted out, have him or her exit the bubble. When the role-play is over, ask students how it felt to be cast out and how it felt to send another to almost certain death. Ask what priorities were used to make their decisions. Discuss how this relates to the way they set priorities and make decisions in their lives today.

Watch Your Step—Form two groups. Have one group think of as many activities as possible that are outside God's will. Have them use a red marker to list each activity on a separate sheet of paper. Tell the other group to use a black marker to write as many activities (each on a separate sheet of paper) as possible that are inside God's will.

Collect the papers from both groups and mix them together. Then scatter them all over the floor. Select a volunteer to attempt to walk across the room stepping only on the activities that are within God's will. Try it a few more times with different kids.

Discuss how this is like trying to follow God's will in their daily Christian walk.

Stumper Stopper—Hand out pencils and paper, and give students a few minutes to anonymously write any areas of life they're struggling to discover God's will in. Collect the papers and read them aloud to the class, one at a time. Have an open discussion with the class to determine what they think God's will would be for each situation. Be sure to have a Bible concordance handy, and always remind the class to consider the question, "What would Jesus do?"

Table Talk—Use the "Table Talk" handout (p. 19) as the basis for a meeting with parents and teenagers. During the meeting, have parents and kids complete the handout and discuss it. As a part of the meeting, play a game together that deals with life issues, such as Life or Choices. After playing the games, ask parents to create "wish blessings" for their kids, by listing several specific blessings or hopeful dreams they have for their kids. Encourage parents to make sure kids understand these are blessings and not expectations. For example, parents may bless their kids' lives with "laughter" or "special wisdom in making life choices."

Polaroid Purpose Party—Form teams of four for a dash-about-town adventure—with a "purpose." Give teams each a Polaroid camera, and have them go in search of things that provide a sense of purpose for different people. Give teams a list of places they must go, such as a bank, a park, a church, a soup kitchen, a school and a suburban neighborhood. In each of these places, have teams take photographs of things that give people purpose in life. Award 100 points to teams for each acceptable photograph. End the trek at a young person's home, where kids can talk about their adventures, and discuss the pros and cons of finding purpose in the things kids photographed.

PARTY PLEASER

What's It All About, Anyhow?—Hold a "mystery" retreat for junior highers at a secret location (the location is a secret from the kids). Present the entire schedule as a quest for kids to corporately discover God's purpose in their lives. Include clues for treasure hunts each day, leading up to the final day when kids discover a huge cross hidden at the retreat site before they arrived. On the cross, write out Matthew 10:39. Finish up the retreat with an honest discussion of how that verse answers the question, "What's it all about, anyhow?"

RETREAT IDEA

CURRICULUM REORDER—TOP PRIORITY

Order now to prepare for your upcoming Sunday school classes, youth ministry meetings, and weekend retreats! Each book includes all teacher and student materials—plus photocopiable handouts—for any size class!

FOR JUNIOR HIGH/MIDDLE SCHOOL:

Accepting Others: Beyond Barriers & Stereotypes
ISBN 1-55945-126-2

Advice to Young Christians: Exploring Paul's Letters
ISBN 1-55945-146-7

Applying the Bible to Life, ISBN 1-55945-116-5

Becoming Responsible, ISBN 1-55945-109-2

Bible Heroes: Joseph, Esther, Mary & Peter
ISBN 1-55945-137-8

Boosting Self-Esteem, ISBN 1-55945-100-9

Building Better Friendships, ISBN 1-55945-138-6

Can Christians Have Fun?, ISBN 1-55945-134-3

Caring for God's Creation, ISBN 1-55945-121-1

Christmas: A Fresh Look, ISBN 1-55945-124-6

Dealing With Death, ISBN 1-55945-112-2

Dealing With Disappointment, ISBN 1-55945-139-4

Doing Your Best, ISBN 1-55945-142-4

Drugs & Drinking, ISBN 1-55945-118-1

Evil and the Occult, ISBN 1-55945-102-5

Genesis: The Beginnings, ISBN 1-55945-111-4

Guys & Girls: Understanding Each Other
ISBN 1-55945-110-6

Handling Conflict, ISBN 1-55945-125-4

Heaven & Hell, ISBN 1-55945-131-9

Is God Unfair?, ISBN 1-55945-108-4

Love or Infatuation?, ISBN 1-55945-128-9

Making Parents Proud, ISBN 1-55945-107-6

Materialism, ISBN 1-55945-130-0

The Miracle of Easter, ISBN 1-55945-143-2

Miracles!, ISBN 1-55945-117-3

Peace & War, ISBN 1-55945-123-8

Peer Pressure, ISBN 1-55945-103-3

Prayer, ISBN 1-55945-104-1

Reaching Out to a Hurting World, ISBN 1-55945-140-8

Sermon on the Mount, ISBN 1-55945-129-7

Suicide: The Silent Epidemic, ISBN 1-55945-145-9

Telling Your Friends About Christ, ISBN 1-55945-114-9

The Ten Commandments, ISBN 1-55945-127-0

Today's Faith Heroes, ISBN 1-55945-141-6

Today's Media: Choosing Wisely, ISBN 1-55945-144-0

Today's Music: Good or Bad?, ISBN 1-55945-101-7

What Is God's Purpose for Me?, ISBN 1-55945-132-7

What's a Christian?, ISBN 1-55945-105-X

FOR SENIOR HIGH:

1 & 2 Corinthians: Christian Discipleship
ISBN 1-55945-230-7

Angels, Demons, Miracles & Prayer, ISBN 1-55945-235-8

Changing the World, ISBN 1-55945-236-6

Christians in a Non-Christian World
ISBN 1-55945-224-2

Christlike Leadership, ISBN 1-55945-231-5

Communicating With Friends, ISBN 1-55945-228-5

Counterfeit Religions, ISBN 1-55945-207-2

Dating Decisions, ISBN 1-55945-215-3

Dealing With Life's Pressures, ISBN 1-55945-232-3

Deciphering Jesus' Parables, ISBN 1-55945-237-4

Exodus: Following God, ISBN 1-55945-226-9

Exploring Ethical Issues, ISBN 1-55945-225-0

Faith for Tough Times, ISBN 1-55945-216-1

Forgiveness, ISBN 1-55945-223-4

Getting Along With Parents, ISBN 1-55945-202-1

Getting Along With Your Family, ISBN 1-55945-233-1

The Gospel of John: Jesus' Teachings
ISBN 1-55945-208-0

Hazardous to Your Health: AIDS, Steroids & Eating Disorders, ISBN 1-55945-200-5

Is Marriage in Your Future?, ISBN 1-55945-203-X

Jesus' Death & Resurrection, ISBN 1-55945-211-0

The Joy of Serving, ISBN 1-55945-210-2

Knowing God's Will, ISBN 1-55945-205-6

Making Good Decisions, ISBN 1-55945-209-9

Money: A Christian Perspective, ISBN 1-55945-212-9

Movies, Music, TV & Me, ISBN 1-55945-213-7

Overcoming Insecurities, ISBN 1-55945-221-8

Psalms, ISBN 1-55945-234-X

Real People, Real Faith, ISBN 1-55945-238-2

Responding to Injustice, ISBN 1-55945-214-5

Revelation, ISBN 1-55945-229-3

School Struggles, ISBN 1-55945-201-3

Sex: A Christian Perspective, ISBN 1-55945-206-4

Turning Depression Upside Down, ISBN 1-55945-135-1

Who Is God?, ISBN 1-55945-218-8

Who Is Jesus?, ISBN 1-55945-219-6

Who Is the Holy Spirit?, ISBN 1-55945-217-X

Your Life as a Disciple, ISBN 1-55945-204-8

Order today from your local Christian bookstore, or write: Group Publishing, Box 485, Loveland, CO 80539.

MORE INNOVATIVE RESOURCES FOR YOUR YOUTH MINISTRY

The Youth Worker's Encyclopedia of Bible-Teaching Ideas: Old Testament/ New Testament

Explore the most comprehensive idea-books available for youth workers! Discover more than 350 creative ideas in each of these 400-page encyclopedias—there's at least one idea for each and every book of the Bible. Find ideas for...retreats and overnighters, learning games, adventures, special projects, parties, prayers, music, devotions, skits, and much more!

Plus, you can use these ideas for groups of all sizes in any setting. Large or small. Sunday or mid-week meeting. Bible study. Sunday school class or retreat. Discover exciting new ways to teach each book of the Bible to your youth group.

Old Testament   ISBN 1-55945-184-X
New Testament   ISBN 1-55945-183-1

Clip-Art Cartoons for Churches

Here are over 180 funny, photocopiable illustrations to help you jazz up your calendars, newsletters, posters, fliers, transparencies, postcards, business cards, announcements—all your printed materials! These fun, fresh illustrations cover a variety of church and Christian themes, including church life, Sunday school, youth groups, school life, sermons, church events, volunteers, and more! And there's a variety of artistic styles to choose from so each piece you create will be unique and original.

Each illustration is provided in three different sizes so it's easy to use. You won't find random images here...each image is a complete cartoon. And these cartoons are fun! In fact, they're so entertaining that you may just find yourself reading the book and not photocopying them at all.

Order your copy of **Clip-Art Cartoons for Churches** today...and add some spice to your next printed piece.

ISBN 1-55945-791-0

Bore No More! (For Every Pastor, Speaker, Teacher)

This book is a must for every pastor, youth leader, teacher, and speaker. These 70 audience-grabbing activities pull listeners into your lesson or sermon—and drive your message home!

Discover clever object lessons, creative skits, and readings. Music and celebration ideas. Affirmation activities. All the innovative techniques 85 percent of adult church-goers say they wish their pastors would try! (recent Group Publishing poll)

Involve your congregation in the learning process! These complete 5- to 15-minute activities highlight common New Testament Lectionary passages, so you'll use this book week after week.

ISBN 1-55945-266-8

Order today from your local Christian bookstore, or write:
Group Publishing, Box 485, Loveland, CO 80539.